Worldwide Membership Cash
Make Money From Anywhere With
Membership Sites

Jack L. Knight

LEGAL NOTICE:

The Publisher has strived to be as accurate and complete as possible in the creation of this report, notwithstanding the fact that he does not warrant or represent at any time that the contents within are accurate due to the rapidly changing nature of the Internet.

While all attempts have been made to verify information provided in this publication, the Publisher assumes no responsibility for errors, omissions, or contrary interpretation of the subject matter herein. Any perceived slights of specific persons, peoples, or organizations are unintentional.

In practical advice books, like anything else in life, there are no guarantees of income made.

Readers are cautioned to reply on their own judgment about their individual circumstances to act accordingly.

Introduction To Worldwide Membership Cash

When it comes to building an online business, there are so many different types of platforms to choose from that it can often become overwhelming and confusing as to where you should begin.

From affiliate marketing, CPA opportunities to developing your own high quality information product, there are many different paths and directions to go.

Out of the many different business opportunities and platforms that I've explored over the years however, one of the most profitable and long-term ventures involves creating high quality membership websites, otherwise known as "continuity websites".

With membership websites, you are able to not only generate recurring payments from every subscriber that joins your website, but you are also able to build credibility within various markets as members recognize you as an authority as well as a source for quality information.

This valuable credibility will provide you with a powerful springboard that will enable you to eventually launch other products, websites and opportunities to an existing base of targeted customers that you have already developed a relationship with.

After all, if someone is willing to pay a

monthly subscription to access information about a specific market or topic, it's likely that they will be willing to purchase other relevant products, or services that serve as components to your main membership site.

However, there is often a misconception that prevents new business owners and entrepreneurs from venturing into the continuity marketplace. They are misled into believing that membership based websites are simply too difficult, expensive or time consuming to create, and maintain.

After all, you first need to purchase a membership script or software that will power your website and help you effectively manage the different areas of your community, but you also need to provide subscribers with fresh, quality content as well.

For many, this part of building a successful membership site is what prevents them from going any further.

But thankfully, it doesn't have to be so difficult.

There are many different ways that you can build successful membership website without having to spend a lot of time or money.

In fact, since membership websites are so flexible in terms of how they are structured, you can build community sites that aren't entirely focused on content at all, but instead, offer training, personal coaching, community access or tools and resources on segments of your market.

This way, you can design your membership website around your preferences, schedule and what you are most comfortable working with.

You could also create a membership website based around monthly updates, so that you are able to free up your time throughout the remainder of the month, while still providing value to your subscribers on a regular basis.

Regardless what market you are interested in catering to, you can build a profitable membership site around that niche, and this report will show you some of the best methods for creating successful membership websites quickly and easily.

So, let's get right to it!

Creating Your Membership Website

Every website begins with a theme. A theme is a specific topic or focus that your membership website will focus on.

While you could create a membership website that carries a broader theme, they are often harder to maintain, and when it comes to creating targeted marketing campaigns, the more focused your membership site is, the easier it will be to tap into your customer base and recruit subscribers to your site.

Before you can choose a theme or topic for your membership site, you will need to conduct a bit of market research, so that you can closely evaluate the viability of creating a membership based website within specific markets that interest you.

While membership websites can vary from small, micro markets to larger mainstream markets, you want to make sure that your topic will attract enough subscribers to make it a profitable venture, while also paying attention to the level of existing competition within your market.

You want to make sure that you can find a 'point of entry', so that you can generate exposure for your membership site regardless of the competition.

There are a few things to keep in mind when evaluating potential topics for your membership site, including:

1) Are there existing membership websites within the market?

You want to build your membership sites around a viable industry, and by determining whether there are successful membership sites already catering to your market, you will maximize your chances of building a membership website that will be widely accepted and of interest to the majority of your customer base.

For example, if during your research you determine that there is a very low number of membership websites that target a specific topic, it's a good indication that the market is too small to accommodate too many membership websites.

While smaller niche markets can be profitable, in order to scale your membership website you want to focus on broader markets.

2) Do you have the ability to provide quality information and resources to this market that aren't already being offered?

Just because you've confirmed that a market is a viable one doesn't mean that you will be able to create a successful membership site for that market, unless you have the ability to create content that your subscribers will be interested in paying for.

Consider the costs of outsourcing content for

different markets, as the more popular a topic is, the greater the number of freelancers to choose from.

If your topic is too focused or specific, you might find it difficult to locate qualified freelancers who have enough experience to produce quality content for your site.

Developing a membership website that offers **specialized content** is a great way to develop a USP (unique selling proposition) so that you can stand out in the market and attract subscribers.

3) How can you offer something new to an existing customer base? (developing your USP)

If you have established that a specific market is actively purchasing and subscribing to similar membership websites, you need to determine your unique point of entry.

How can you create a community of your own that offers something different than what other membership sites are offering? How can you offer distinct value in your own membership program?

You need to set yourself apart from other membership sites in the marketplace by first defining your USP, and then creating a membership website that clearly demonstrates how you are different, how your members benefit by being part of your community, and why they should choose you over the competition.

Your USP could be as simple as the delivery methods that you offer, or the format in which your content is made available.

For example, if you find a competing membership website offering ebook-only products to their members, consider offering both ebook and video or audio based versions of the information products that you create. Since people prefer to learn in different ways, by offering many different formats for your training tools, you are able to cater to a wider audience while separating yourself from the competition.

4) Is your theme or topic considered "evergreen"?

Evergreen topics include subject matter that will still be in demand years from now.

These topics aren't based on fads or temporary hot topics, but rather on stable, long-term markets that have proven to be viable over a long period of time.

Markets that are considered evergreen include weight loss, parenting, employment, finance, credit, health topics and even sports or hobbies.

It's important that your membership site is designed around a viable topic so that you can build a **long-term membership program.**

After all, you want to focus on a scalable

community base that can consistently grow and maximize your overall income, and if you base your membership website around a short-term topic, you will struggle to retain subscribers after the initial buzz wears off.

Another important thing to keep in mind is the overall size of your target market.

You want to make sure that your membership site will attract enough subscribers to justify the time and work involved in consistently updating the community with fresh content.

Here are a few other things to consider:

1) Will you be able to come up with fresh ideas for future updates to ensure that

your website stays fresh?

2) Is your market scalable with the potential for ongoing growth? Can you offer upgrade options to further maximize your income, or are products and your overall scope extremely limited?

3) Is your target audience able to solve their problems quickly (making it difficult to retain subscribers), or is your potential topic able to expand so that you can cater to a large-scale, ever-growing community?

These are just a few things to keep in mind when choosing your membership theme.

Once you have a general idea as to your membership theme, take it one step further by identifying what you are personally interested in or experienced with that could add additional value to your community program.

- Are you experienced with a specific instrument?
- Are you trained in specific programs or software?
- Are you experienced with popular hobbies or sports?
- Are you knowledgeable regarding a specialized topic in a 'desperate' market?

The best membership sites involve frequent activity from the administrator so the more active you are within your membership community, the easier it will be to develop a relationship with your subscriber base and encourage member loyalty.

This means that you want your membership theme to be something that you are personally interested in or have experience with. You'll also find it easier to develop content for your site if you have a genuine interest in the topic.

Also keep in mind that themed membership sites are always much easier to manage and monetize than generic communities. You want a strict focus on your membership community, so that you can expand on the topics, yet retain an overall theme.

The more focused your website is, the easier it will be to tap into your niche market and determine exactly what your target audience is interested in and provide it to them. If your membership site is too generic or broad, you will have trouble tailoring your content to what the majority of your members base is looking for.

If you struggle to pin down a topic for your membership website, consider exploring the digital marketplaces where you can quickly evaluate potential topics and see what is currently selling.

One of the greatest resources for evaluating potential membership site topics is found at http://www.ClickBank.com

While ClickBank is primarily known for digital products, they also showcase membership based websites from within dozens of categories and niche markets. You can locate membership websites by searching using the *"Future $"* option within the search area of their marketplace.

You want to search through existing membership sites and communities in order to determine how their membership site is structured (traditional, coaching based, email based, etc), their price structure, whether they have an affiliate program, as well as the specific content that is being offered and overall value on the site itself.

Then, ask yourself the question:

"How can you improve on their existing model?"

Can you expand on the topic's coverage and provide additional resources, tools and information?

Write down any ideas that you come up with as you evaluate existing membership sites in your niche market, for future reference.

This will help you thoroughly analyze the existing subscription sites in your niche so that you can create an improved membership website, that offers unique value to your own members base.

Another simple strategy for reviewing potential markets and topics for your

membership site is by exploring
www.Amazon.com to determine the number
of available products focusing on your
subject matter. This is a great way to
determine whether or not your market is a
popular (and profitable) one.

SPYFU, available at http://www.SpyFU.com
is a great niche research tool that will provide
detailed statistics on keywords as well as
existing Adwords advertisers.

Google Alerts is an exceptionally useful tool
for locating hot topics and current trends
that could serve as potential ideas for your
membership site. You can access Google
Alerts at http://www.Google.com/alerts

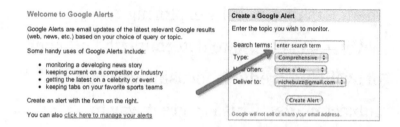

Yahoo Answers and Yahoo Buzz are also two very useful research tools that will help you come up with killer membership topics based on overall popularity.

With Yahoo Buzz, available at http://www.Buzz.Yahoo.com you are able to keep on top of current trends and hot topics.

All of this research takes a bit of time but it's a critical step in effectively evaluating the theme and topic of your membership site so that you can build the very best membership website possible within your market.

When creating your membership website, there are many different models that you can choose from, including coaching or training, email based courses, monthly updates or you can even choose to set up a "time limited" membership site, where subscribers pay to access training materials or weekly courses for a limited time.

In the next chapter, we'll take a close look at the different options available to you so that you can choose the best format for you, and begin building your membership website!

Choosing Your Membership Model

When it comes to building your own membership website, you have a few different options in terms of exactly how it's structured and designed to operate.

For example, depending on your goals, you might want to create a membership website that is short term, where it's designed to offer content on a sequential basis, until the cycle ends, and then the subscription is terminated, and re-starts as new subscribers sign up.

This is particularly common with e-mail based courses, where a subscriber signs up at a flat rate and receives weekly ecourses in their inbox for a period of time (usually

30-90 days). Once the eCourse finishes, the subscription cycle ends and the subscriber is no longer charged for access to the training.

On the other hand, if you are interested in developing long term membership programs, you may want to focus on the traditional platforml, where members pay a monthly subscription fee to access content or resources, where the membership program never ends unless the subscriber chooses to terminate their subscription.

To help you evaluate the different membership models, let's take a closer look at the most popular platforms for some of the most successful membership websites today:

Traditional Membership Platform

With a traditional membership website, your subscribers pay monthly for regular content updates and new releases.

By far, this is the most common method of building a membership website, however it does require more frequent updates than other membership types.

In many cases, traditional membership sites either offer a low trial price with the cost increasing once the trial is offer, as a way of generating interest and encouraging visitors to explore the websites offer. (this is also a great way to stand out from the competition in the event they are not offering a no-risk trial).

Example: A subscriber would be given the

option to join the membership site for only $17 for the first week (7 days), then $37 monthly, set on a fixed term rate. This means that even in the event you increase your prices later on, charter members who initially took advantage of your introductory offer, are locked in, and are not required to pay any additional charges or increased fees.

This structure is a very successful one, and can really help your membership website get off the ground, as you are providing a clear incentive to subscribers, as well as encouraging members to stay subscribed to your website so that they can continue to receive access at a lower rate than future subscribers.

Traditional membership sites are usually

updated on the 1st of every month, but one savvy technique is to update halfway through the month so that subscribers don't join at the end of the month only to gain access to two months worth of content.

You should also consider setting up an archive section of your website, so that new members are able to purchase previous releases or updates, rather than gain access to everything. Remember, your subscribers are paying for monthly access to your content so it's only fair that you value their subscription by limiting content on a monthly basis. Anyone who joins your website halfway through a month should only be able to access the current months content.

Traditional membership sites can be set up a number of different ways, customizing everything from the delivery format, to the update schedule. It's your website, so make sure that you evaluate the different options and choose a platform that works best for you based on the time you have to allocate to your community, as well as what you believe your members would prefer.

One thing to keep in mind is that when you launch your membership website and begin to generate subscribers, it's often difficult to switch formats or change delivery times, so make sure to do your best to carefully plan out your website early on, so that there is no need for abrupt changes.

Believe it or not, your subscribers will come

to rely on the schedule that you implement into your website, and in order to retain consistency and demonstrate your desire to provide a stable, ever-growing community, you need to do your best to thoroughly plan out your entire membership program before it even launches.

Coaching Based Membership Website

Coaching based training programs typically offer members the opportunity to receive training or personal assistance for a flat fee, although there are membership based coaching sites that charge on a monthly basis for continued access to new training modules or lesson plans.

With a coaching based membership site, lessons are accessible only to members of the site, with schedules being made available for all members in regards to meeting times, personal coaching sessions and live calls.

Coaching may include:

- ✓ Personal training (one on one sessions)
- ✓ Group Session Training (forums, conference calls etc)
- ✓ Forum Based Training
- ✓ Ecourse Training (delivery of lessons via email)

You need to be objective when analyzing your member base, so that you can create a tailor made training program suitable for specific segments of your market.

For example, your training program will need to address a specific skill, or experience level so that you can ensure your members can understand and apply the information you provide during the course. You want to be very careful to first survey what kind of help potential members are interested in, so you can gauge the overall demand and interest and create a laser targeted coaching program.

Coaching based membership websites are extremely easy to set up because unlike traditional membership websites where you'll need to develop and publish content prior to your website launch, with service based membership websites, you can update your website less frequently, creating content and resources only as the site grows.

Email Based Membership Programs

With an email based membership program, you are able to set up complete membership sites quickly, with very little start up costs or work involved. After all, since the majority of the content will be delivered via email, you don't need a dedicated server, or expensive membership software to manage your program!

You will also want to determine a delivery schedule, making sure to send out the newsletters on the same day each week, for consistency.

When it comes to frequency, the most common formats include eCourses sent weekly, bi weekly or monthly.

When you are deciding what your publishing schedule will be, keep in mind the kind of information you will be supplying to your membership and its *"dated importance"*.

If you are offering information that changes quickly or regularly, then you are going to want to consider sending out your ecourses more frequently, perhaps even implementing a RSS feed into your course, so that members can receive instant broadcasts of new updates.

If your information is evergreen and unlikely to change quickly, you can set up a weekly or even monthly e-course, where subscribers receive a new module or lesson through email on a regular basis.

ECourses are exceptionally profitable, because you can minimize the workload involved in launching your membership program. You will only need a professional autoresponder/email delivery account, such as http://www.Aweber.com or http://www.GetResponse.com, the first month of content, and a way of accepting payment for each subscription.

The easiest way to set up an email based membership website is to create a simple subscription page that features a subscription button (You can create these directly within your Paypal account). When a visitor to your site decides to enrol in your ecourse training, they can either choose to subscribe to a monthly payment plan, where they receive one new module every month, or perhaps a one-time flat fee for the entire training series.

Choosing Between Free & Paid Formats

The obvious benefit of a paid membership program is the monetary element, however, setting up a free membership program can be just as rewarding.

Here's how:

With free memberships, the foundation is usually based on allowing free entry with the intention of selling a membership upgrade. Using teaser options like this, you initially attract a customer with a no obligation, no cost offer. In other words, you eliminate the risks involved and instead of forcing a visitor into making a quick decision to join your site or exit your page, you are able to capture their information, add them to your database and follow up at a later date, in the event they failed to upgrade right away.

The free membership module works very well if you have the ability to create quality content on the front end to wet their appetite, and work towards encouraging subscribers to upgrade for access to even more information or resources.

Building a subscriber database from free membership accounts may seem less profitable than charging an entry fee on the front end, however by capturing leads you will have an opportunity to communicate with them through follow up emails later on, encouraging them to upgrade their account for full access to your material or resources.

It's said that the average visitor needs to visit a website up to 3 times before deciding to purchase a product, and by offering them free entry on the front-end, you eliminate lost sales while building a laser targeted mailing list!

We've just covered the most common membership formats online. Consider which format will work best for you, and let's move onto the next step, choosing the software that will essentially power your entire membership website.

Note: If you plan to create an email based membership program, you can skip the next chapter and move onto *"Creating a Polished Membership Site"*.

Finding The Right Membership Software

In order to set up your membership site, you will want to evaluate the different membership scripts available on the market and choose the one that will offer you the most flexibility.

Membership scripts are an important part of a successful subscription site because they handle everything from payment processing, to ensuring that your content is delivered on time, based on your programs schedule.

Membership scripts also make it easier for you to effectively manage and update your website, as most professional membership scripts come bundled with everything from user management tools, to powerful administration options that help you to keep your membership site up and running efficiently.

You want the membership script that powers your website to be flexible, scalable and able to handle a large amount of data. That way, you don't have to worry about any problems later on, when your membership site grows.

Depending on the membership script you choose, many of the most feature laden scripts on the market not only power your membership website, but actually come bundled with CSS based templates, so that you can easily edit the header and footer files and upload a feature-rich website in just minutes.

Before you choose a membership script for your website, you need to identify what kind of offers you plan to implement into your community program, so that you can purchase the right membership script to get the job done.

For example, certain membership scripts only protect user areas, but fail to provide you with the ability to offer one time offers, up-sell offers or integrate a backend system into your website.

Just the same, certain membership scripts only allow for one level membership packages, while others provide you with the option to set up multi-level programs, so that your subscribers can upgrade their accounts to access additional areas.

Depending on how large or detailed your membership site will be, you may need different functionality from your membership script, so spend some time evaluating the different options on the marketplace, taking advantage of any demo sites, or trial offers available, and choose the one that works best for you.

If you aren't sure how to develop or design a membership website, consider using Wordpress as the CMS (Content Management System) to organize and manage your entire website.

With amember.com, you can purchase modules that will seamlessly integrate a membership script within a Wordpress blog, forming a bridge between the main (guest) area and the areas only visible to paying subscribers.

Regardless of the software that you choose to power your membership site, there are a handful of features that you will most likely want to make sure are included, even if you don't intent on using them right away, chances are, you will want to implement them later on in order to maximize your income.

This includes:

1: Timed Release Content

With timed release content, you are able to create and schedule posts, pages and updates so that they appear on scheduled times and dates. This is exceptionally helpful in planning out your updates and in saving time by publishing content in advance and setting it to appear only on the day your site updates.

2: Unlimited Membership Levels

Your membership site software should offer you the option of creating various levels (Bronze, Silver, Gold, etc) so that you can offer extended upgrades and upsell offers to your subscriber base as your website grows.

For example, you could offer "Group A" with access to certain areas of your site for $9.97, while Group B can access all of the areas that Group A can, as well as extended resources, tools and content areas for $19.97 per month.

Having the ability to assign levels is also important in the event you want to feature a temporary offer or a special update that is not part of your regular membership program.

Then, you can advertise the offer to your subscribers and allow them to purchase access for a limited time.

3: Sequential Content Delivery

Depending on your setup, you may want to graduate your members from one level to the next. For example, a member joins your site today and receives access to one module. Then, your sequential delivery system would deliver the next module only after the subscriber has been active for a week (or another period of time).

This is a great way to build a training program that automatically delivers content based on where, in the training, your subscriber is.

4: Autoresponder Integration

It's very important that you are able to capture your visitor and member's information so that you can send follow up emails, promotions and frequent updates of when your website has been updated or in the event you are promoting a special offer or time limited bonus.

List building is an essential component in being able to community with your members and in maximizing subscriber retention. The more frequently you communicate with your subscriber base by offering new features, releases and updates, the more likely your members will remain active.

It's also a good idea to notify your member's base of an upcoming update, in the event you plan to archive the previous months release. That way, members have the chance to download or view the content before it's pulled from the site.

You can also use this email system to survey your members' base to determine what they are interested in receiving with future updates. This information is incredibly valuable in order for you to create a membership program tailored towards your target audience, and to ensure that your subscribers remain active members!

5: Integrated Affiliate Program

You also want to make sure that your membership script offers the ability to run an affiliate program, so that you are able to encourage members to promote your website while earning commissions.

Most membership scripts come bundled with a ready-made affiliate program, where you can choose to make all members affiliates or you can allow members to choose to enrol in your affiliate program.

By offering members a commission for every

new subscriber they refer to your site, you will able to maximize your websites exposure and build a massive customer base, with very little marketing of your own! If you've done a great job at delivering quality content, your members will be more than happy to promote your site, and what better way to generate new interest than from satisfied members?

6: The Option to Scale Your Website

You need to make sure that the membership software you choose will allow for your community to grow, and is equipped and able to handle large amounts of data and frequent activity. Not every membership script is powerful enough to handle a lot of database activity, so be careful to choose a membership solution that has been

thoroughly tested and proven to
accommodate large membership
communities.

One quick and easy method of building full-scale membership sites is by integrating membership software into a Wordpress based website.

This way, your website will be fully optimized for the search engines, while you are able to benefit from a full featured content management solution. If you aren't experienced in developing websites or fiddling around with HTML code, setting up a Wordpress based membership site removes all of the tedious work or time consuming learning curve!

In order to bridge your membership content and seamlessly integrate it into a membership access portal, I suggest using a

membership based script exclusively
designed to integrate with Wordpress.

Wordpress Membership Scripts:

www.WPWishList.com
Features unlimited membership levels,
flexible options, sequential content delivery,
control viewed content, shopping cart
integration and more.

www.MemberWing.com
With MemberWing, you can instantly set up
a membership website using nothing more
than Wordpress and this simple plugin.

Tasks that take a lot of time to do by hand
can b e handled automatically with software
and that will free up a lot of your time to do

the creative things that make your website profitable.

Once you have chosen your membership website's theme and software, you will need to register a domain name and set up a hosting account that will house your subscription center.

www.NameCheap.com and www.HostGator.com are both affordable options.

Just make sure that you choose a memorable domain name that truly represents your niche market. You want people to remember your domain and have little trouble spelling it. You also want to utilize keywords whenever possible not only to attract targeted visitors, but to help your website rank within the search engines.

If you have trouble coming up with a domain name, head on over to http:// www.InstantDomainSearch.com where you can enter in keywords to determine what domain names are available for registration.

Creating A Polished Membership Website

Your membership website will generate a steady income from within its own community based on your chosen platform, however in order to maximize your income you should begin to develop a back-end system so that you can increase the value of every subscriber.

Consider how you can integrate different options that would appeal to your members, or integrate various levels into your membership community so that active subscribers are given extended options or benefits by upgrading their accounts to access different areas of your site.

Consider creating up-sell offers, one time offers or other back-end offers that compliment your membership program, and add extra value.

For example, you could consider setting up a membership site that offered various levels, starting with Bronze, then upgrading to Silver and finally Gold. Each level would gain access to extended content, special downloads or exclusive offers.

Another method of thoroughly monetizing membership websites is that rather than offer a front end system that is based on a recurring fee, you could instead, offer a flat rate access fee with upgrade options.

For example, your membership site could be

priced at $97 entry fee (one time charge) with a monthly rate of $67. What this does is help in customer retention, because if a subscriber cancels their account, they would then have to re-subscribe, paying $97 again before being given the monthly discount rate.

You should also consider using *urgency-based strategies*, such as time sensitive offers, or limited quantities or spots left within your membership community.

You could also consider offering coupon codes, with only a specific number available before expiring. This will motivate your visitors to take action and subscribe before the offer ends.

When it comes to membership websites, there are a few things you will want to integrate into your system in order to maximize your profits, and retain subscribers.

One easy way of enticing visitors into becoming paid members is by offering what is known as 'teaser content", which showcases snippets of content on the main website in order to entice a visitor into becoming a paid subscriber.

Sites that provide information to find work-at-home jobs, for example, can see the listing of jobs but cannot apply for the jobs unless they are members of the membership site itself.

You will also want to pre-determine your content schedule. This way, you can stay on track with updates and your subscribers will know exactly when to expect new material. If you ever have to change your update schedule, always notify your members so they are aware of any changes.

Here are some other ways to further enhance your membership site:

Feature An Affiliate Program

You will also want to incorporate an affiliate program into your membership website, so that both visitors and subscribers are able to generate commissions from every referred sale they make.

When structuring your affiliate program,

focus on offering a very appealing commission percentage; in order to recruit active affiliates who will help you jump-start your marketing campaigns.

Different companies pay different percentages and amounts for leads and sales. The differences paid for a sale can range from 75% down to 1% depending on the company and the product.

What you decide to pay your affiliates will depend entirely upon what you are selling and to whom you are selling it. A good idea would be to check what other companies selling a product comparable to yours is paying their affiliates.

However, how much you pay your Affiliates really depends on how much your product/ service costs, its profit margin, how much you're willing to give up and what action you want to take place.

When running an affiliate program, you will want to make sure that your current membership script or software is able to effectively track all sales and leads, as well as provide detailed information to affiliates (including overall earnings, stats, payment dates, etc).

You could also actively join affiliate programs that are focused on your niche market yourself, and incorporate your affiliate links into a "Recommended Websites" page, so that you are able to maximize earnings by promoting third party products and related websites.

For example, if you run a membership based website focusing on golf training, you could feature affiliate products that include golf gear, advanced lessons, physical books and even video tutorials.

This way, you can maximize your income by featuring affiliate-based tools, resources and materials that you are not offering yourself, without having to advertise competing membership websites.

Just make sure that the products or services you are recommending are relevant to your overall theme.

Sell Ad Space Within Your Members Center:

You could also consider offering advertising space within your member's center, once your subscriber's base has grown.

This way, you could monetize "un-used" space within your member's center by allowing third party merchants to promote their products and services to your community.

If you run a members forum, you could also consider integrating promotional banners and allocated ad spaces that feature affiliate based products.

If you run a newsletter (and you should), you could also offer solo ad campaigns to advertisers who are interested in gaining exposure at affordable rates.

Just be sure to adjust your advertising prices as your community grows and your overall ad campaigns become more valuable.

List / Email Promotions:

Apart from allowing advertises to purchase email based advertisements, you could also monetize your subscriber mailing list by sending out promotional emails that showcase affiliate products, as well as your own special offers.

Consider creating a special bundle that features new content, relevant to your membership site, and making it available as an upgrade only to existing members.

Renewals: Recurring income is one of the best parts of running a membership website, and something that many other types of online businesses lack.

Just remember, while first time subscribers certainly breathe life into a membership website, renewals keep it alive.

Make sure to consistently remain active within your community and to do your best to provide high quality, exclusive material to your subscriber base on a regular basis.

When it comes to building a profitable, highly monetized membership community, you need to remain consistently active. This doesn't mean that you need to dedicate every hour of your day building your community, in fact, you can outsource the majority of the work to experienced freelance writers and developers, but what it does mean is that you need to play an important role in defining your community.

The more you engage with your community, and the more you communicate with your subscriber base, catering to their interests and expectations, the easier it will be to effectively grow your community, while retaining subscribers for an extended period of time.

Give your members a true feeling of community spirit by incorporating a forum, live chat, or weekly tele-conferences, and engage and interact with your subscriber base, so that they feel connected to the community.

Whenever possible, always power up your membership site with your own unique, proprietary content, rather than with private label or saturated content. The more exclusive and original your material is, the more valuable it will be to those who pay to access it.

Running a profitable membership website takes time and energy, but it can be exceptionally rewarding if you dedicate yourself to consistently evaluating your community and what it is interested in.

Don't be afraid to survey your members to determine what they are most interested in, and would like to see added to the membership program.

After all, it's their community!

Launching Your Membership Website

The easiest way to jump-start your membership website is by creating a mailing list of those who are interested in the same topic that your membership site is focused on.

To begin, you should set up a registration process so that whenever a visitor lands on your website, you are able to capture their name and email address, adding their details to your mailing list (via your autoresponder).

The reason why this is so important is that, once you have their information added to your database, you will be able to send out follow ups and broadcasts in the event that they failed to sign up on their first visit.

This is how it works:

Your visitor enters in their information via your membership site's main page (or individual squeeze page) and confirms their request to be added to your newsletter.

You could consider offering an incentive such as providing a discount code sent via email immediately after each subscriber confirms their request to join your list.

Once a visitor subscribes to your newsletter, your autoresponder kicks in and emails your prospect a welcome email that provides more information about your membership site, as well as the incentive offer that you advertise on your squeeze page (example: membership coupon, special bonus, download etc)

Your autoresponder continues to email your subscriber on pre-set dates, according to the system you have set up within your autoresponder account. You are in full control of how often you email your subscribers, and can continue to add new content into your autoresponder system as often as you like!

Example: You create 5 emails that are scheduled to be delivered accordingly:

1st Email: instantly sent to your subscriber thanking them for subscribing to your list and provides the offer that you are featuring on your squeeze page or landing page (such as your coupon, download product, etc).

2nd Email: Scheduled to sent out on the third day after your subscriber has confirmed their request, and includes an email offering free content, additional articles or another report.

You should also remind subscribers who have failed to register for a paid account, that their coupon code is set to expire if they fail to use it within a specified time frame.

3rd Email: Scheduled to go out on the 7th day of the sequence, and once again reminds your prospect how they will benefit as a paid member of your site.

You could offer additional free resources, including an overview sheet of the features and benefits associated with your subscription site. You could also consider offering a discount access coupon on a higher level package.

4th Email: Scheduled to go out on the 10th day.. and so on.

The balance that you use when mixing up free content with promotional based material is entirely up to you, however the more value you give to your list, the easier and faster it will be to develop a relationship with your subscribers, so that they trust your recommendations and look forward to receiving future broadcasts. It will also help minimize subscribers from opting out of receiving your emails.

It's up to you to keep a pulse on your subscriber base, and determine what works best, how frequently you contact them, and whether they respond well to the products you are promoting.

Just don't be afraid to experiment and test out new ideas and innovative ways to consistently grow and maintain your subscriber base.

Social Marketing

You can generate a lot of traffic to your membership website, with establishing a reputation within your niche through social networking communities. While this traffic strategy does take a bit of time, you will find it incredibly easy to set up and manage your accounts and campaigns.

There are literally hundreds of different social networking websites available online, with the most popular communities being:

With Facebook, you can interact with those in your market by adding them as a contact, but you can also generate exposure a number of other ways from within the Facebook community:

Facebook also offers an internal advertising channel, where you can set up PPC or CPC campaigns. Facebook offers extensive customization options including the ability to define your advertising schedule, as well as target specific segments of your market based on gender, age and even location.

You can create your advertisement by visiting http://www.Facebook.com/advertising

You can also begin generating exposure by creating a "Facebook Fan Page" that allows potential customers and subscribers to join your fan page, and receive instant updates and alerts each time you publish new material to your page.

With Ning, you can create your own private or public social network, allowing members to view article content, resources and tools posted to the community channel. You can also limit visibility only to members, encouraging visitors to join your social network prior to gaining full access to your material.

Twitter is the leading social network and information portal online. You can quickly establish an online presence, generate targeted traffic and even build a mailing list by submitting regular broadcasts, growing a following and using free tools including to schedule automated broadcasts that are sent out to everyone who chooses to follow you.

Create Powerful Backlink Campaigns

There's a lot of buzz around building quality backlinks in order to boost search engine ranking, and generate organic, targeted traffic to your membership site.

There's a good reason for this;

Backlinks count as "votes" for your website and the more you have of them, the greater your exposure will be within the major search engines.

Backlinks identify the value of your website, and the source as well as quantity of backlinks signify to the search engines, just how relevant your website is.

This means that it's important to focus your back-link building efforts, on both obtaining a high number of backlinks as well as quality backlinks that link to your site from established, relevant websites and blogs.

There are a number of different ways to build an effective backlink campaign including generating backlinks from authority blogs, communities & forums!

When it comes to generating back-links from authority blogs you simply spend time posting comments within open threads, using anchor text (when possible) to link back to your website using relevant keywords.

While not all blogs provide "do follow" links, (meaning that the link will count within the search engines), it's relatively easy to locate blogs that offer link juice.

One of the easiest ways of finding relevant 'do follow' blogs is by downloading the free Firefox plugin, available at:

https://addons.mozilla.org/en-US/firefox/collection/seo-tools

In addition, you can use the free Comment Hut software to pinpoint blogs based on keyword and customized search terms to quickly locate relevant blogs in your niche market (all of which offer do follow backlinks)

http://www.CommentHut.com

<u>Article Marketing</u>

Article marketing is an incredible marketing strategy regardless whether it's for a high end product or in building a mailing list, and if executed correctly, it can be the primary force behind generating consistent traffic to your membership website.

Article marketing is extremely easy to set up, and even if you aren't a proficient writer, you can easily outsource article creation to affordable, high quality writers.

Even if your budget is very small, there is no reason why you can't compile a small package of articles, spanning from 300-500 words in length that are highly targeted and relevant to your squeeze page's topic.

The greater the number of articles in circulation, the more exposure you will receive, however you always want to focus on producing high quality content, rather than just on the quantity that is being distributed between these networks.

Since articles are available for re-print, where webmasters can use your content on their websites and communities, (as long as the Author's resource box is left intact), you will also be able to build additional back links from the websites that feature your content throughout their network.

Start out by submitting 3-5 articles every

week, and before you know it, your article campaign will generate consistent traffic to your squeeze pages. As you continue to expand on the number or articles in circulation, you will be able to generate more traffic on a regular basis.

Just make sure that the articles you do submit into article directories are exceptionally well written and targeted.

After all, these articles represent you and your brand, and you want your readers to be impressed with the quality as they are likely going to base your other products on the information found within your article content.

Here are the top article directories that you should focus on submitting content to:

http://www.Buzzle.com

http://www.EzineArticles.com

http://www.GoArticles.com

http://www.ArticlesFactory.com

http://www.WebProNews.com

http://www.ArticleDashboard.com

http://www.ArticlesBase.com

http://www.ArticleRich.com

http://www.Articles-Hub.com

http://www.SubmitYourNewArticle.com

http://www.Articlesnatch.com

The most important thing to remember is that you need to create a compelling Author's Resource box as this is the area where you are able to include a link to your website and direct readers to explore your own personal site.

Since the space allocated is quite limited, you need to focus on using a strong call to action that prompts the reader to click your link and visit your website.

The best way to go about creating your Author's Resource box is to think of it as a short commercial, where you are given a very limited time to explain the benefits and highlight the most important features of your product or service.

In addition, if you offer a freebie or giveaway within your Resource Box, rather than a direct pitch (such as directing your reader to download a free report or ebook by visiting your squeeze page), you will instantly maximize your articles performance in terms of driving targeted traffic to your websites, as well as in building relevant mailing lists of potential buyers.

Tip: Be sure to include your primary and long tail keywords within your article's content itself, so that your article content appears within search results for both the main search engines like Google.com, as well as via the internal search utility on the article directory websites.

Video Marketing

With video websites like YT it's never been easier to use the power of viral video to generate fresh traffic to your websites. All you need to do is develop a video or slideshow presentation that highlights your giveaway and directs people to your squeeze page.

Better yet, you could incorporate video tutorials based on your niche market, with a direct link to your membership website that appears at the end of the video.

That way, rather than setting up video marketing campaigns that only offer a promotional slideshow, you are adding value to the community by offering useful information that your target audience will appreciate.

Like article content, search engines rank video pages individually, so if you upload a video that receives a good amount of exposure, you will benefit from a higher search engine ranking as well as the direct exposure from the video community itself.

Pay Per Click Marketing

One of the easiest ways to create an automated traffic system and jump-starting your membership websites launch is by harnessing the power of pay per click marketplaces, like Google's Adwords.

In case, you are unfamiliar with what PPC entails, here is a brief summary of how it works:

Visit http://www.Google.com and enter in any keyword phrase you wish, such as 'Acne Solutions'.

The advertisements that appear under the 'Sponsored Listings' on the results page are PPC advertisements, as shown above.

Advertisers can create as many advertising blocks (and campaigns) as they wish and by bidding on keywords, their advertisements will appear within different positions.

When it comes to developing the highest converting PPC campaigns, your keyword research is an important part in ensuring that you are effectively targeting the right keywords based on your niche market.

These keywords should be highly relevant and speak directly to your potential customer.

Google uses a proprietary system called the Quality Score.

The QS examines a number of different factors in order to figure out whether the page you are sending traffic to matches the keywords you are bidding for.

In addition, your quality score is determined based on your overall campaigns preformance, so the higher your CTR (click through rate), the lower your cost per click will be.

This means that you need to ensure that you are using highly relevant, targeted keywords within your PPC advertisements.

Quality Score Factors Include:

- CTR for the keyword and the ad
- Overall CTR of your entire account
- The CTR of your display URL
- The quality of the landing page
- Relevance of the keywords to the landing page
- Relevance of the keywords to the ad

You want to make sure your landing page matches the keywords you choose very closely.

When creating your advertisement within

your PPC administration panel, you will need to assign specific keywords to each ad block. Start off with 5-10 keywords and gradually add in additional keywords as you begin to see progress with your PPC marketing.

This way, you won't become overwhelmed with trying to monitor and manage exceptionally lengthy keyword phrases and will be able to determine which ones are best performing, and which ones you should remove.

Remember, keep your keywords grouped tightly, use multiple landing pages when necessary, and test and track ads continually, always working to improve your CTR and conversions.

*Create your PPC Account at http://
www.Google.com/ads*

Bookmark Your Membership Website

Here are the top 10 social bookmarking
websites for generating fresh back links and
quality traffic to your site.

All of these websites contain DO follow,
ensuring links leading to your website will
count within the search engines as a valid
back link:

1 - http://slashdot.org (PR9)

2 - http://digg.com (PR8)

3 - http://technorati.com (PR8)

4- http://www.furl.net (PR7)

5 - http://www.backflip.com (PR7)

6 - http://www.hugg.com (PR7)

7 - http://www.mixx.com (PR7)

8 - http://ma.gnolia.com (PR7)

9 - http://www.connotea.org (PR7)

10 - http://mystuff.ask.com (PR7)

CPSIA information can be obtained
at www.ICGtesting.com
rinted in the USA
LVHW010507140521
687424LV00006B/610